Trade Against the Trend!

Heikin Ashi Trader

DAO PRESS

Table of Contents

Part 1: The Snapback Trading Strategy

Chapter 1: Trade when the crowd is afraid 4

Chapter 2: Why I do not follow the trend 13

Chapter 3: Mean Reversion 15

Chapter 4: Risk Management 26

Chapter 5: How do I recognize extreme movements? ..30

Chapter 6: Patience at the entry 37

Chapter 7: Does the Stop really protect me from heavy losses? 42

Chapter 8: Trade Management 46

Chapter 9: Exit 47

Chapter 10: When do the best trading opportunities occur? 49

Chapter 11: Why you should study the economic calendar 50

Chapter 12: Which markets are suitable for the snapback strategy? 55

Chapter 1: Examples in the Stock Indices 57

Chapter 2. Examples in the Currency Markets (Forex) 60

Chapter 3: Examples in the stock markets 63

Chapter 4. Examples in the commodity markets 67

Glossary 70

Other Books by Heikin Ashi Trader 74
About the Author 77
Imprint 78

Part 1: The Snapback Trading Strategy

Chapter 1: Trade when the crowd is afraid

"I believe the very best money is made at the market turns. Everyone says you get killed trying to pick tops and bottoms, and you make all your money by playing the trend in the middle. Well, for twelve years, I have been missing the meat in the middle, but I have made a lot of money at tops and bottoms."

Paul Tudor Jones

Anyone who starts trading on the stock market should be fearless. I do not say callous, I say fearless. If you want to win as a trader, you have to be willing to take trades that hardly anybody dares to take. It has been like that forever. If you do the same thing as the rest of the herd, you get what the herd gets: almost nothing.

Therefore, if you want to do something crazy, like trading, then it should be worth it. Anyone who has read my scalping books knows that I am a countertrend trader. That means: I wait until a trend is exhausted and then take the opposite position. As a scalper, it just seems logical to me to try to trade the turning points that Paul Tudor Jones talks about in the quote.

This setup has convinced many scalpers. However, many, like me, have seen in recent years that it was not always easy to find markets where you could scalp well. The method works best in bear markets. I developed the method especially for such times.

In long-lasting bull markets, as has been the case since 2009 (as of November 2018), volatility will continue to dry up. So, it is getting harder and harder to find a market where you can scalp well, using this method. Therefore, many scalpers have begun to trade according to classic day trading methods. They trade on a 5-minute or even a 15-minute chart. Others have started using my method on higher timeframes. Of course, it also works there, because it is based on the universal principle: the best opportunities are at the turning points.

Do any alternatives exist for times of low volatility? One of these is the **snapback strategy**. What is this? Everyone knows that if you stretch a rubber band, it will snap back eventually. In addition, the more you stretch the band, the stronger the backlash will be. This principle also applies to the stock market. That is why we speak of "snapback", that is, the band is snapping back after a movement has been stretched in an exaggerated way.

This method is based on the assumption that when a market makes an extreme move in one direction, one can assume that a backlash will follow. Although it is hard to anticipate the preceding movement, the trader can expect a counter movement, with a high probability. The snapback trader relies on this probability. He does not even try to guess if a market will make a big move up or down. He waits patiently.

If he perceives such a movement, he positions himself in the opposite direction as soon as the preceding movement stutters or shows signs of weakness.

Fig. 1: Bitcoin, weekly chart 2016 – 2018

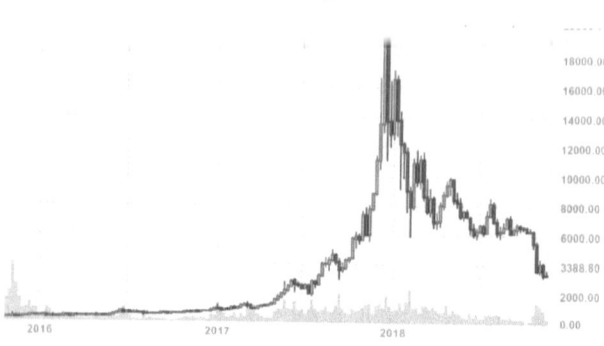

In figure 1, you see the example of a market that was stretched quite far. It literally crashed after it had shot up like a rocket, as if there were no limits. At least, that was what the optimistic crypto traders thought, dreaming of even higher prices.

This chart reminds me of the times of the dotcom bubble in 2000. Thousands of new "traders" also appeared out of nowhere, thinking that the laws of gravity had been rejected. Any experienced stock trader knows that it is only a matter of time before the house of cards collapses. That was the case after the dotcom bubble. It happened with the crypto-currencies, and it will always be like that where a market screws up, as if Newton's laws suddenly no longer apply. This phenomenon is the topic of this book. I want to explore market situations that are just screaming for the rubber band to snap back.

Anyone who read my scalping books will recognize the setup. I am one of those traders who does not try to predict major market moves (a specialty of analysts). I cannot predict such movements as much as I would like, so I certainly do not try. What I can very well expect, is that after an extreme movement, I usually can expect a countermovement, a correction. My method builds on this logic.

There have always been traders who have been trading with the snapback method, or a variant of it. For example, some traders specialize in trading extreme moves in smaller stocks, so called penny stocks. Especially, if those traders are capable of going short in "overhyped" penny stocks.

Newsletter writers like to recommend certain penny stocks for their readers. They impress the readers of the letter with a very positive story about this small company. The readers call their broker and buy all the available stocks, which usually cost only a few cents on the stock market. That is why they are called penny stocks. Of course, it gets tight quickly in such a tiny "market". Soon the readers will buy up the order book of this stock completely. The result is, the stock starts to rise massively. Price increases of 100 or 200% within two or three days are quite usual. Such an exaggeration inevitably brings snapback traders, who specialize in shorting such stocks, onto the scene. They try to build short positions the moment the momentum in the stock ends. Everybody has bought and is sitting on profits. The first ones are starting to take their profits, putting the stock under pressure. When the short sellers enter into the stock, more pressure comes in. Not infrequently, the stock crashes completely, often even deeper than where it was a few days earlier, when the stock was recommended by the newsletter. Needless to say, clever snapback traders are the ones who are making a decent profit here. Not the "readers – investors". However, they have to be careful, because they may be wrong with their timing, and the stock might go up further for a while. If, in this case, the snapback trader does not take his losses quickly, he may experience a bigger loss.

There have always been scammers (quite often the publishers of those penny stock market bulletins themselves), who had previously bought the stocks before they recommended it in their stock market letter. When their "readers-investors" start to buy, they change suddenly to the seller side. That way, they benefit twice. No, three times. First, they make money with the subscriptions of their stock market letters (a profitable business!). Then they make money when the stock starts to rise. Finally, yet importantly, when the house of cards collapses, they often make money by building short positions. These people actually trade against their own readers of their stock market letters. Most of this happens through some straw men.

This practice is illegal. There have been spectacular condemnations in the past. Moreover, although everyone knows that regulators can identify this kind of fraud, surprisingly, there have always been individuals who have done it. If you want to know how it works and have some fun, all you need to do is watch the movie "The Wolf of Wall Street" with Leonardo DiCaprio. This movie shows how well this practice works. However, the film is set in the eighties, where the "dummies", so the "readers-investors" of the news bulletin, were lured on the phone. Of course, today it happens via email. But the principle has always remained the same.

Anyway, this book is not about penny stock trading and certainly not about illegal practices. Rather, I want to show the reader how to benefit from extreme movements as well, provided he overcomes his fear of doing the opposite of what the herd is doing.

For example, if a market runs to the north for seven hours, and there are the first signs that the buyers are running out of cash (losing momentum), then you can be sure that I am on the other side of the trade. I am short. And honestly, doing this is scary. Sometimes you might be a little bit scared, sometimes really scared. I am no exception. I am scared too. If the whole market is long, and you have a short position, then you really feel that you are alive.

Conversely, it is the same. If the market has fallen all day due to some event, and everyone is short, then you can assume that I am long. And this position scares me too. *Me against the rest of the world*. That is what this book is about: **Me against the rest of the world.**

I would not talk about these snapback trades if I did not believe there is a robust trading strategy behind this method. Otherwise, what I am sharing here would be worthless. I would like to make it clear again, that this method is not my invention, but has always been used by smart traders worldwide. Maybe you have not heard of it yet, because those people do not make a fuss about their business. These traders have internalized the method of taking the opposite position of extreme movements, so that they no longer have to think about it. They go short just when the mass of traders do not even dream of going short; if they go short at all (we know that only 1% of investors go short at all).

Most people just need some kind of "confirmation" that the market has turned and that they should now trade in the other direction. Some might say they need "a signal" to go long or short. There is an entire stock market industry that thrives on delivering such "signals" to inexperienced traders. If you intend to subscribe to such a "signal service", you will lose on the longer term. Believe me, I tried it several times in my early days and always fell on my nose.

Why? Because when the "signal" comes, the opportunity has already gone. Those signals usually come too late. Think about it: first, the analyst must recognize the signal on the chart. This happens when his indicators give him one. This is mostly when the market has already turned and has gone a bit the other way. Then the analyst (who, by the way, does not act on his own signals - he leaves this to the readers of his signal letter) goes to the computer and begins to write an exciting report, stating that his indicators have given him a significant signal. As a rule, some hours have already passed. If he then writes his report in the mailing list, and finally clicks on "send", several hours have passed before you get the mail. Depending on the size of the signal service, the readers start to buy and eventually, so do you. Think about it. Not everyone is at the start of the food chain.

The reader may already guess it. If you always wait for confirmation, the caravan will already have moved on. If you get into the market then, you usually get a much worse price than if you had bought, for example, when the market was completely down. That is self-explanatory, one should think. The old German stock market expert Andre Kostolany summarized it aptly: "You have to buy when blood flows in the streets." Actually, this saying is the expression of common sense itself. The questions I ask are: "Why is it so hard for traders to put this stock market wisdom into practice? And why are many traders so scared to buy when blood flows in the streets? And why are so scared to go short when the rest of the world is long?"

The claim that I make in this book is simple, but very direct: <u>if you do not experience fear when trading, then the position is probably not worth taking.</u>

In other words, *trade only when you are scared*.

Some traders may take my approach for granted. They should not. You would wonder how many traders buy or sell at points in the chart that are irrelevant. That is why I say: trade only when you feel afraid.

For people who are not used to trading, such an assertion could seem absurd. How can you risk money on the basis of fear! However, that is exactly what it is all about. If you only have a little experience on the stock market, you know that things are not rational here, as economists and analysts would like it to be. The stock market is often crazy. Almost every day, you can experience some kind of exaggeration. And that is exactly what real traders make their money with.

If the stock market were a rational entity (as the stock market engineers, as I call them, suggest), then there would be no reason to enter it. Because then every price that the charts indicate would be a rational price and justified by the so-called fundamental data. Then the *market efficiency hypothesis* would have won. The market efficiency hypothesis states that stock market prices reflect all the information available in that market. Everyone who has only a bit of trading experience knows that this is not the case.

However, the question is not: "How do you subdue this irrational thing called the stock market?" That is what the stock market engineers are trying to do. They design strategies based on back testing, that are spat out by their computer programs. There is nothing wrong with that. I have developed some myself, and I have written a nice little book about it. I know this way of thinking well and respect the traders who choose this way.

I wrote this book for traders who are more inclined to listen to their instincts. If you learn to listen to your gut, you can have the same success on the stock market as someone who calculates the whole thing and then runs it from a computer program. I would like to ask that the lady and gentleman engineers leave the room now. Those who I call the "crazy traders" can stay. These are the traders willing to do things the masses of traders never dare to do. In other words, from now on, we are going to talk about those trades where you get really scared. For as the Roman poet Plautus said: *Abducet praedam, qui occurrit prior.*

(Latin: The early bird gets the worm)

Chapter 2: Why I do not follow the trend

Buy high and sell higher or sell low and buy lower. This is the mantra of trend followers. It sounds like common sense. Usually, that is what almost the entire trading industry recommends constantly. Reason enough to be skeptical.

The problem is, trend trading does not work for most traders. Now, you could blame me for trying to trade lows and highs at a mere guess. For who knows where the high or the low of the day or the week will be? Nobody.

That may be true. However, that is why switching to trend-following is just as much "guessing" for me. Because the assumption that the market will continue in the current trend direction, is just a guess. How could I know for sure?

For me, traders who want to follow the trend act subliminally even out of fear. They want to feel "safe" in the herd, because the herd follows the trend. It is always safer, or it feels safer when you go with the crowd, so, with the trend. Since the masses are on the safe path, and are afraid of being noticed, the results of this path are generally mediocre as well.

The best you can expect if you go this way, are moderate profits. That is why I say that if you want to among the winners on the stock market, you will have to look your fear in the eye. You will have to learn to walk a lonely path and you will surely have to learn to act against the majority of traders.

That is why I am a contrarian, a trader who acts against the trend. I am a trader who goes long when the whole world is short and vice versa. This is uncomfortable and certainly not for everyone. That is why it is important to understand why my countertrend method works. I would like to explain this in the next chapters.

Chapter 3: Mean Reversion

Before we get into the details of this trading method, we should first consider the reason why trades can work against the trend and why it is less risky than it seems at first glance. We are talking about the *mean reversion effect*. The term comes from statistics, in which it is better known as "regression toward the mean". It describes the often-observed phenomenon that after an extreme measurement, the subsequent measurement is once again closer to the average, if chance has an influence on the measured variable.

What sounds complicated is actually something simple. It means that the further away the measurements are from their average, the more likely they are to return to it.

In terms of financial markets, this theory implies that markets that don't correct themselves over time, not only by chance, tend to exaggerate. Markets, so to speak, have a "memory" and tend to reverse previous movements.

Specifically, this means that any price increase must be corrected at some point (i.e. it must be replaced by falling prices). Simply put: "What goes up, must come down" and vice versa.

Mean reversion, or returning to the mean, means that in the long term, prices do not just fluctuate around a medium level - they also actively return to it. The theory is therefore in contrast to the already mentioned market efficiency hypothesis.

The idea behind mean reversion is that prices that are "far" from the mean will eventually return to it.

A trading strategy based on mean reversion is based on the expectation that extreme price changes will have to return to their previous mean value. Of course, this applies to both extremely high prices and extremely fallen prices.

Many, as you know, there are different technical analysis indicators, based on this assumption. The best known among them are the RSI (Relative Strength Index) and the various stochastic indicators.

Although many trading strategies rely on these indicators, or use them for signal generation, they have proven to me to be inadequate when it comes to generating profitable trading signals. The error rate is just too high, no matter how you change the parameters.

The reason for the "failure" of these past databased indicators is simple. What statisticians describe as an average is not static. It is also by no means permanently fixed, so that the trader only needs to "wait" for prices to approach that value again. You might end up waiting for a long time, and the wait might even be in vain.

As an example, average returns on fixed income securities may apply here. The statistical average is historically around 3%. However, the yield has been far below that since 2010 and investors had to wait a long time before the yields came closer to their "historical mean". In plain language, this means that mean values are not static quantities that are fixed forever, but dynamic variables that are influenced by external effects, such as inflation. Average values are therefore "moving" price targets, which of course makes it difficult to calculate them exactly.

If the mean value of fixed income securities remains reasonably stable at 3%, it looks very different in a market such as crude oil. Here, the statistical average has been $ 31 since 1960. We have moved a long way off from that time and again, and the question is whether we will ever see that value again, though it is not impossible. If the largest oil producer in the world, Aramco from Saudi Arabia, at some point finally get their IPO, then we could soon see rates well below this mean value, because then the oil sheiks would have to put their cards on the table and tell the whole world how much oil they actually have. If this were to happen, and it turned out that the Saudis have enough oil to fill all the world's oceans (which is not unlikely!), we could quickly see a price of $ 31 for crude oil, and much lower prices too. So, be careful with overhasty opinions about the price of oil.

This brings me to an encounter that I had several years ago, with an American trader who was visiting Berlin. When I heard what he was doing, I invited him to a restaurant, and he gladly accepted. He was a friendly, but discreet man, who did not make a fuss about his job. He looked at me in surprise when I asked him if he could explain his trading strategy to me. I was the first in his 30-year career who was interested, he said. "How can that be?", I asked? He said that everyone else either wanted to sell him something, or to give him his opinion about the markets. No one was interested in what he did. I was obviously the first person to ask him about his method.

I spent four hours in a Berlin restaurant with this trader. He could hardly believe that I just listened to him. From time to time, I asked him a little question for clarification, which he gladly answered. You will not find anything about this person on the internet or anywhere else. He does not have a website, nor does he need "advertising" to find customers. On the contrary. Since he is older, he is starting to think about quitting and he is more worried about getting rid of his customers. In his case, that is not so easy. He knows each customer personally and he is even friends with some of them. He also goes to the trouble of meeting with each one of them once a year to discuss the development of their accounts and their financial goals. He has dozens of customers and some have been with him for decades. Two of them were among his first customers, and have remained faithful to him throughout all those years.

This trader makes an annual return of 10 to 15%. There have been hardly any loss years, or none at all. No wonder his customers were satisfied. That is why he does not need "marketing". With this person, all of his business comes by word of mouth. And he has more customers than he would like to have. Despite his success, he remains exceptionally modest.

Of course, the accounts vary in size. Beginners may have $ 50,000 or $ 70,000 with him. Others have entered with larger sums. He also has several accounts of several million dollars because they have grown so much over the years. This trader has made several millionaires during his career. Some have actually dissolved their deposit with him and since then, they have been living as private individuals from their well-filled pensioner's account.

This person is, for me, the best example of what someone can achieve in the longer term, if he consistently and unerringly applies a particular method.

But, by the standards of most hedge funds, or even by the standards of Wall Street, this trader is perhaps just a small number.

However, do not get me wrong. If he manages modest "capital accounts," that does not mean his income is modest too. On the contrary. Since he makes his money through a profit share, he has an exceptionally high income, money that his customers are very happy to give him.

And the amazing thing is, that in order to perform this activity, he does not need any special structures, legal or otherwise. "Didn't you set up a company for your activity?" I wanted to know. He shook his head. He would have had more work with a company. He needs his time for the customers, whose accounts he monitors individually. Every morning he sits down for a few hours, opens the account of one of his clients, and looks to see if he needs to change anything. He actually thinks about every single account of each and every customer. "Everyone has his or her own financial goals," he told me, "and I have to consider them."

Because he deals with one specific account daily, he usually gets through all his customers in a month. When the month is over, he starts all over again with the first customer. At the annual meeting with each customer, he always takes notes. He not only knows exactly the financial goals of each customer. He also knows all about their families. He knows if someone has died or if there is a new grandchild. He knows if someone is ill or on the way to recovery. In short, this trader knows his clients and thinks about each one individually.

Now, you are probably wondering which particular strategy this trader has. It is very simple. This trader trades mainly with ETFs. He does not trade individual stocks, but he observes a basket of international markets and sectors. For example, he could build positions in ETFs that map the telecommunications sector, or buy an ETF on oil producers or US utilities. He is also very aware of international events. If he sees a chance in Turkey, because stocks have fallen sharply there, then he buys an ETF on the Turkish stock market.

His strategy? He buys when a market has fallen 20%. Period.

That is the whole strategy.

"What?" I asked. "Is that all?"

He looked at me with a puzzled look. Yes, he said calmly. That is all. He could not understand that I did not really understand what he meant.

"But," I said, "what do you do if the market drops another 20%?" "Well," he said, "then I buy again. I buy when the market drops 20%." "But that's "averaging down,"" I said. "Sure, it is," he said, and he looked at me again in amazement. Until then, I had considered averaging down or cost averaging, as one of the biggest trader sins ever. He looked at me as if he did not quite understand what I had a problem with. He had no problem with that. It was his method. You buy a market when it is cheap. He did not care if he had to wait two months or five years before the position went into profit. He was patient enough and so were his customers. If the market falls 20% again, great! Then he just buys again.

Since he works without leverage, he can simply wait out any losing position. He also does not consider loss positions as such. He just says: "I have a position." He knows that time is on his side.

It works for him. Since he does not trade equities, but only markets, his position can never go to zero. No matter how bad a sector is, at some point every bear market is over, and then his courage pays off. He considers this to be normal and he has the time to wait for this moment.

I have rarely seen a more modest and laidback person than this trader. He has no excessive return expectations. If it is "only" 5% in a given year, that does not make him unhappy. This trader survived the 1987 crash in the SP500. He survived the bursting of the dotcom bubble and the 2008 financial crisis. He has been involved with all the bull markets and bear markets since the 1980s and has piloted his clients' accounts through these ups and downs. And every time, he bought when the market had fallen 20%.

Why am I telling you this story? First, of course, because I admire this trader for what he has achieved and still does today (he wants to remain anonymous). I learned more in those 4 hours in the Berlin restaurant than in many years trading on the stock market. This trader breaks almost all the rules that the conventional trader's knowledge is trying to point us to, and he is very successful.

He does not use stops, for example. He looked at me again with that peculiar expression when I addressed the subject. At that moment, I was not sure if he even was familiar with the term "stop" ... For him "having a position" was about the same as "having a conviction". Of course, that was another rule he broke, because the all the trading literature is full of statements that you should not have a conviction. If possible, also no opinion. This trader acts just the opposite way. "I think Turkey will recover from this crisis and stocks will rise again," he said, when I asked him why he had just bought an ETF on Turkish stocks.

Thus, when he bought Turkish stocks, it was because of a clear opinion he had about the Turkish stock market. If he was convinced that a market was undervalued, due to a correction or an unforeseen event, he was interested in building a position in that market. And he did not care if that market continued to fall after he had established an initial position. "All the better," he said, "Then I can get them for even lower prices."

Thus, he violated another "golden rule" of the conventional trading industry: never averaging down. This rule is probably one of the holiest cows that was invented by this industry. This rule is based on the strange assumption that a trader always has to be right with his first position. If not, the stop ensures that he limits his losses. Since this happens quite often, the trader just has to make several attempts. Of course, that suits the brokerage industry perfectly. More trades (a stop order also leads to commissions) mean more revenue for the broker. One should be careful whose literature one reads...

This trader was not a good customer to his broker. If he bought, he did not care if the position was in his account for a week or five years. With such an attitude, as a broker, you are not going to make much money from this kind of trader. He was just thinking too much about his customers and far too little of his broker's sales.

He has never attended a brokerage fair or a conference of hedge fund managers, even though, technically speaking, he leads one himself, and he does so very successfully. He only goes to New York occasionally, when he wants to take a flight to Europe. He loves to spend weeks in cities like Rome, Paris or Prague and visit as many museums or art exhibitions as possible.

New York and Wall Street do not interest him at all. He prefers to meet with one of his clients and speak about his children or grandchildren. He knows exactly who is doing well and who is struggling with health problems. He does not look at the money at all, because he has enough of it. On the contrary. He confided in me, that he would prefer it if more clients would close their accounts, because then he could spend more time in Europe. Yes, this trader manages his "fund" on the go, with a simple laptop.

He has plenty to do and he does not want to be involved with the trading industry or Wall Street. When he is at home, he lives in a medium-sized city, somewhere in the middle of nowhere. He is a completely unique person who does his own thing and does not care about any rules. He is, for me, the personification of the American dream. However, it is not the dream of somebody who enriches himself at the expense of others. He has earned his freedom and money through consistent and honest work. He does not promise you the blue of the sky. He explains to every investor what he can expect: a solid return with a long-term strategy. And honestly, that is exactly what most people who do not trade want. Just think about it.

At first glance, this story does not have much to do with the strategy presented here, because unlike my friend's method, the snapback trading strategy is short-term, actually, very short-term. If working with this strategy is to work, you have to use stops, as always when trading in leveraged products. I am telling you this story, because I want some of the equanimity of this American trader to rub off on you, because you will need it.

If you plan to trade by the snapback method, or any other strategy, you will soon find out that the most important habit you need is equanimity. This trader has it. He is not scared either. When a stock or a market falls 20%, most traders are scared. This is an unfamiliar situation. As long as markets go up and down one or two percent, the world seems to be in order. However, if a market crashes 20% or more, then everyone is afraid, because it could get worse. Sometimes it does. My trader friend is not scared in that kind of situation. His whole method is based on waiting until such an event occurs. Then he acts. And he does it methodically, calmly and in complete serenity.

You may be wondering how you can achieve such serenity, because there is always something exciting about trading with leveraged products. That is for sure. But the longer you trade, the more you will long for that equanimity. At some point, you will want to be able to sleep peacefully and not have to constantly think about the positions that you currently have in the market. And you can only do that when you start thinking about <u>the size of your positions</u> today. And that is exactly what we want to do in the next chapter.

Chapter 4: Risk Management

As every trader knows, or should know, risk management is one of the most important, if not the most important tool in his toolbox. The trader should be the one who controls the risk and not some external factor like "the market" or worse, his undercapitalized account.

The latter, in my experience, is the biggest reason why traders fail: over-leveraged positions. What do I mean by that? Inexperienced traders take positions (on margin, that is, on credit), which are downright ridiculous in relation to their trading capital. I am serious. Ridiculously big! I know that many traders use the so-called 1% rule. However, I think this rule is still risky. If you risk 1% of your capital per trade, that might not seem like much to you. If you lose once, you still have 99% of your capital available (though mathematically this is not correct, in fact, you have less).

Professional traders risk 0.2 or 0.3% and sometimes even less. The reason is simple: you can trade in a much more relaxed manner with this kind of position. If you are in a drawdown period, it does not kill you. If you have a lesser period with your 1% rule, then losing 10% or 15% of your trading capital will start to nag your confidence. You will become unfocused or worse, you will start to take bigger risks to make up for the accumulated loss quickly. That is human, but it is the guaranteed path to total loss. Believe me; I know what I am talking about. I destroyed several accounts myself, trading this way. Several!

So please, do not copy me. Get it right at the beginning and start reducing the size of the position you intend to trade. Halve it, or even better, trade with a quarter of the original size. This makes it much easier to trade and live. This applies in particular to the method presented here. From time to time, you will find that the market is going against your position much longer than you expected. Yes, markets can sometimes move insanely irrationally in one direction, before correcting (see Bitcoin and co). If you are on the wrong side of the trade, sweat forms on your forehead more quickly than you can imagine, an unmistakable sign that your position is too big. It is better to make sure that you do not get into this situation in the first place.

Now, some readers may object, all well and good, Heikin Ashi Trader, but if I trade with such mini-positions, then I barely advance my account, let alone make enough to be able to live off my trading.

My response to this objection is categorical and straightforward: get the idea out of your head of ever being able to make a living from your ridiculous $ 10,000 "trading capital." You will not succeed.

Your task is first to master your chosen trading method. Specifically, if you are able to earn a return of 15 to 20% on a yearly basis, like my trader friend, with maximum drawdowns of less than 10%, then you are damned good. With my relaxed risk management that is doable.

Therefore, if you have the ability to achieve such star yields with manageable risks, then investors will give you all the money in the world. Because investors are looking for just that: a robust annual return with manageable risk. How do you get this money? I explained this in my book "How do I start a trading business with $ 500".

Forget about achieving that goal with your measly capital of $ 10,000 (or even less). If you want to achieve this ill-advised goal, one thing is certain: the professional traders will get that $ 10,000 even faster than you can imagine. I know that most traders will ignore my advice (I did). However, do not say that I did not warn you.

I have another tip. Let us assume that you have $ 10,000 trading capital. Please, only transfer 20% of it, i.e. $ 2000, to your trading account. If you made a profit of $ 200 or $ 500 after some time, transfer this money to a checking account, i.e. an account that is not intended for trading. Reward yourself. You cannot make a living out of this, but you will program your subconscious mind to success. So do not think in percentages, but in real money. Money you can spend (a nice meal, a visit to the movies with your beloved or, as I do, some expensive cigars).

Let me say it again clearly: if you plan to make a living with such a small sum, get it out of your head. This tiny starting capital, no matter how much it is, serves to help you learn your craft first. If you still get the crazy idea that you can make a living by trading your own account, then you should bring at least half a million dollars to the table. With this capital, you can give it a try with conservative risk management (after sufficient preparation and training). I do not recommend it, not as long as you have not mastered your craft.

If, like most people, you do not have this money, so you will have to convince investors to give it to you. You will only be able to do that <u>when you are actually able to trade</u>. That means, that you have built a track record that is at least a year old and that meets the criteria that I mentioned earlier. Then, you might be on your way to becoming a real professional like my trader friend.

Everyone goes his own way. Of course, you can try to qualify for a hedge fund or any asset management. It is possible, but it is not easy, I know what I am talking about, because I have walked that path myself. Alternatively, maybe you can try my trader friend's method. This is actually the most appealing to me. A lean structure with the least possible administrative costs and a personal relationship with your customers.

Oh, and about the earning potential of such a model... My friend easily earns a middle six-figure sum. Yearly. I do not know your ambitions, but I could live on this kind of money very well.

I do not want to rule out that you can still succeed "on your own", in making a million out of $ 5000 or $ 10,000. There are individuals who actually became big traders from modest beginnings. They exist, but there are not many of them.

Chapter 5: How do I recognize extreme movements?

In order to recognize an extraordinary movement, it is important that you see the move in the chart in the right perspective. That means that you should not only look at the current movement, but <u>you should compress the chart</u> so much that you can see the movement in the context of the past days or weeks. Only then does the importance of the current movement become clear, and you can begin to assess whether what is currently happening is an extraordinary movement or not.

Image 2: Gold, hourly chart

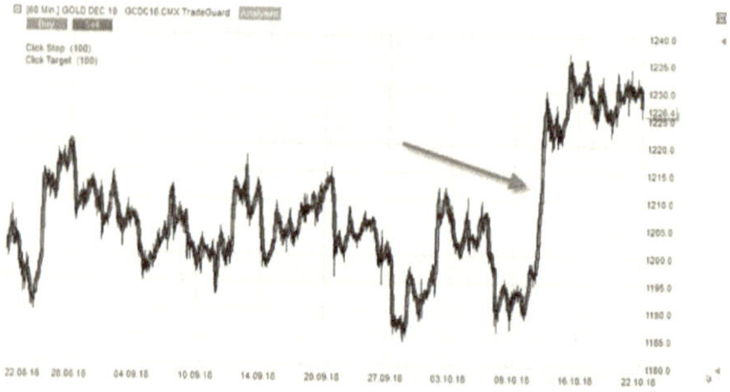

What I mean by compression is best illustrated by this hourly chart in the gold future. I try to make as much data as possible visible on the chart while compressing. You can clearly see that the upward movement on the right side of the chart (arrow) stands out from the rest of the price movement in the weeks before. In a few hours, gold rose more than in the whole month before. Movements like this should catch your attention.

I found another example in the German Bund Future (futures contract on German Government Bonds with maturities of 10 years), which lasted several days and gave the future more than 600 points in profit.

That was a big move at the time. Why do I know that? Because I put the movement in relation to what happened before. Look at the price before the move and compare it to the upward push that followed (green arrow).

Figure 3: Bund Future, 4-hour chart, December 2017 - June 2018

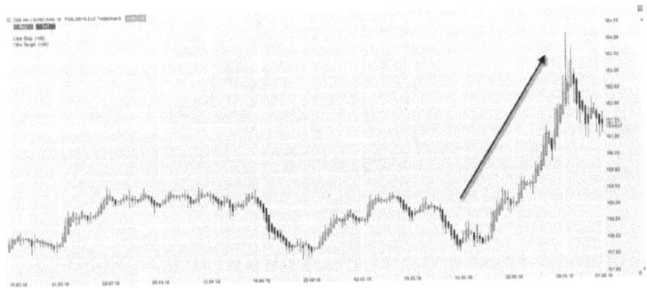

The price action before this move was relatively calm compared to this move. The future moved, with the exception of the downward movement of 5-7 March, in relatively quiet tracks. On most days, the trading range was less than 70 points. Then, suddenly the future rose over 600 points within a few days.

Of course, there are usually "reasons" for such a change in the market. However, that should not interest us here. As we said before, it is difficult, not to say impossible, to predict or anticipate such outliers. What we usually can expect, is that such extreme movements will eventually be corrected. In this example, the upward move was even corrected to more than 50% and a short seller could make a decent profit here. Incidentally, the Bund Future returned to exactly where its classic "Mean" was previously, i.e. the average price of the last 50 days, better known as the 50-day line (green line in the chart in Image 4).

Image 4: Bund Future, daily chart, February - August 2018

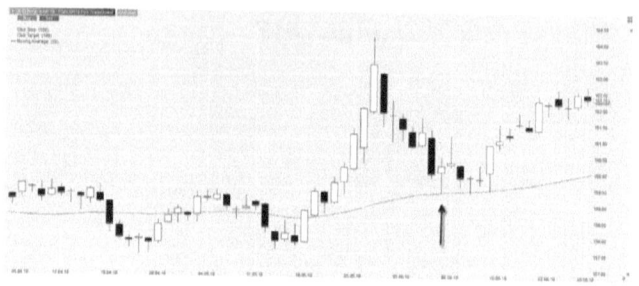

The Future temporarily "moved away" from the 50-day line (green line in the chart) and then returned to it, almost exactly as if nothing had happened (black arrow below).

The image also illustrates that there is no such thing as a static average, as already mentioned. The green line that represents the 200-day line goes along with the general trend of the Bund Futures. It will rise if the Bund Future prices are higher and it will fall if the majority of the bunds go down. I will not go into the topic of whether to weight a moving average exponentially. For the snapback trading strategy, which is a short-term strategy, it does not matter or it hardly matters. I could not see any improvement in the results when

I used an exponential moving average instead of the simple moving average. It is up to the individual trader whether he wants to use the 200-day line or another indicator in this strategy. Of course, the 200-day line (in the daily chart!) gives you an indication of what the professional players in this market currently consider a "fair" price. However, as I said, this perception is also constantly changing. The line may be helpful, for example, if you want to set a price target, if you bet on the mean reversion principle. In this example, it would have worked out very well. It should be clear to the reader that this is not always the case.

Let us take a look at this movement in Bund Future again, this time in the hourly chart, because then you will notice a special feature.

Image 5: Bund Future, hourly chart, May - June 2018

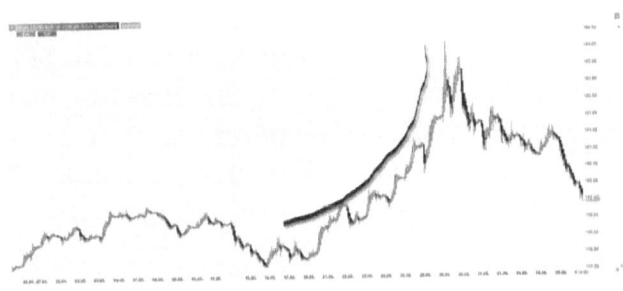

If we take a closer look at the picture in Image 5, we see a typical market situation that will attract the attention of a snapback trader. At some point, the market began to break out. This did not happen explosively, but gradually. The upward movement started on May 18, 2018. At first, it seemed to be a normal upward movement, which took place in the context of the usual price movements of the previous weeks. However, after the weekend on Monday, May 21, the upward movement continued. In the following days, there were always minor corrections, but at the latest after a day, the buyers drove the market higher and higher. At some point, it seemed like there would be no end to this rally. On Monday, May 28, the future started off with a gap downward. However, the buyers closed this gap in a few hours. Then they pushed the market up further. They effortlessly scored 150 points that day and the closing price was almost the high of the day. The next day, Tuesday, May 29, finally, the bulls were out of whack. They drove the Bund 200 points higher within three hours. Anyone who opened the hourly chart of the Bund Futures at the time could follow the almost rocket-like upward movement.

Those who kept track of the past few weeks could clearly see in the chart that the future was in the process of making **a parabolic move**, similar to the one we know from the Bitcoin chart. The characteristic of such a movement is that it increases exponentially. At first, the movement seems to be "normal", but gradually the prices rise more and more, until they shoot almost vertically upward, as was the case on the morning of May 29. It almost seems like the market is going through the roof.

This is usually a sign that the mass of traders is exclusively long and there are no sellers. That is exactly the situation that calls the attention of a snapback trader. You only have to wait for the first signs of weakness in such a market. It is usually the moment when the first traders begin to realize their profits. Because, the way in which the Bund shot up in the first trading hours of May 29 was almost no longer "normal", although such a statement in the stock market is somewhat dangerous. Theoretically, the future could have gone hundreds of points higher. You should always expect such an eventuality, especially on such crazy days. That is why it is so important that you really work with hard stops for this strategy. There have always been situations in the past, where markets have gone on irrationally, as if the actors involved have lost all sense of "reasonable prices". Protect yourself against such a situation.

When the extreme movement will finally weaken, is difficult to predict, and you can at any time – at least in the short term – expect further increases (in the case of an upward movement). These then also constitute the greatest danger to the contrarians who are short. They are "grilled", as the traders like to call it. Therefore, an active stop setting is essential for each contrarian. He has to limit his losses, knowing that the momentum can overrun him at any time. That is why I do not recommend this method for a beginner. Only those traders who are able to assess such market situations and who are able to choose an appropriate position size should consider it.

Nevertheless, every "sly fox" out there on the markets licks his lips when he observes such a parabolic movement on the chart. He knows from experience that it is only a matter of time before this trend turns, or at least corrects itself. As soon as the market prepares itself to make more highs, the stops have to do their work. This would unequivocally show the contrarian that he is wrong in his assessment and that the moment has come to get out while the loss is small.

Of course, this clearly illustrates that you will also have losses with the snapback method. As with any strategy, those losses are logically related to potential gains. You can therefore reduce trading to the simple formula:

hit ratio / average profit - average loss.

By understanding and mastering this formula, you will be able to build a profitable trading business, no matter what strategy you intend to trade.

Chapter 6: Patience at the entry

As already mentioned, it is not easy to determine when a market is oversold and thus justifies the opening of a short position. We should try to understand the concept of overbought – oversold in the context of current market events. For example, if a market is in a strong trend, that concept will become obsolete. A rapidly rising market is permanently "overbought". That is why all the indicators that relate to it fail here. In return, of course, dips or technical corrections in a strong uptrend are undoubtedly good buying opportunities. However, this is not the subject of this book.

That is why I do not work with indicators to determine my entry. They do not help me. <u>My money management helps me</u>. And it is, as already discussed, rigorously conservative. It must be, otherwise I could not reach my goal. If you keep the positions small enough, they remain manageable. That is what it is all about. You should never lose control of your position, no matter what happens. If for some reason you lose control, you should close the position immediately or at least reduce it.

Nothing is carved in stone with this method. The snapback trader tries to catch the highs and lows. However, he will rarely succeed. As a rule, he will find that he got in "too early", and in some cases, of course, "too late." Therefore, you must and should assume <u>that your position will initially be in the red first</u>. In some cases, alright. The usual approach then is to "limit the losses", so to work with stops that are relatively close to the entry. Small losses do not hurt, it says.

This may apply to scalping strategies and most day trading strategies. The snapback method is neither scalping nor day trading nor a swing trading strategy. Because sometimes you will realize your profits after 20 minutes, sometimes only after four days. And you have to be able to bear that.

Conventional day trading usually relies on exact timing, which cannot really exist. Anyone who has ever tried it knows this. You have either bought too early (the market continues to run against you) or too late (the market has already turned and has already corrected itself somewhat).

When using the snapback method, I always recommend viewing the chart from the point of view of a higher time level. I usually look at hourly charts, which I compress to keep track of what has happened in the market over the last few weeks. If you use a higher perspective, you will eventually see the ridiculousness of your anxiety when your position is at a loss first. You just bought and the market has dropped another 50 points. So what?

I hope you understand now why you should trade with small positions. In general, the power of mean reversion will eventually strike, and the market will revolve. If you have too large a position in the market, relative to your capital, and you have to close it because you can no longer "bear" the losses, then you cannot profit when the market turns and begins to run into your advantage.

One of the biggest hurdles for aspiring traders is patience. Well, let us face it. Who has that? Can you open your trading platform in the morning, study your charts, then close the platform, and not make a trade? You do not trade, because there is simply nothing to trade. The markets do not provide an opportunity to trade according to the snapback strategy. All markets are running smoothly within their usual range. There is no extreme movement on any of your charts that gives the reason for a trade.

If you can muster the patience and discipline to wait for the few real opportunities in the week, you will be able to significantly increase your chances of success. In my experience, on average, every week, there are two or three excellent chances if you limit yourself to the main markets. If you use a scanner to search for extreme moves in stocks (at least 15% minus or more), then maybe a few more.

The quick profits that you sometimes can and must take (see examples in the second part) sometimes give the impression that you would have scalped the market. However, for me, scalping is something else (see my book: "Scalping is fun!").

I am convinced that with this method, you can build a profitable trading business. You really do not need more than 40, 60 or 70 points every now and then. And you do not even have to sit in front of the computer screen all day long to get those gains. On the contrary. Once you have set your scanners correctly, a short check may be enough every three hours. After a while, you will see if there is a trading opportunity or not. The modern mobile devices make it a very easy. Some platforms even send you an alert (SMS or e-mail) when something interesting is going on in the market.

This method has the advantage that it does not require you to trade all day long in order for it to work for you. At the same time, you can do other things (or trade other strategies).

Incidentally, this also applies to the times when you have a trade in the market. Do not make the mistake of following every tick of your trade here. Trading is a probability game. You will never catch, or only by luck, the high or low of the day. That means that your entry into the trade is just a coincidence. Of course, the snapback strategy is based on the market correcting the previous move, at least partially. How much correction the market will make and whether it even will correct itself is best left to the market.

In other words, <u>you should always work with bracket orders</u>. Bracket orders always consist of three orders. If you want to go long, open the position with a buy order. This order is automatically accompanied by a sell stop order, which determines your risk in the trade. At the same time, the system also sets a sell limit order. This is to secure the profit once the market reaches your target price. This bracket order is a function of your risk management. It serves to calculate your maximum risk. If, for some reason, you are no longer able to watch the trade because of other commitments, the bracket orders will do the work for you. Either the market will catch your stop or the price target. However, it could happen that you are still in the position when you come back. Then you have the opportunity to realize the accumulated profit and close the order. No one obliges you to wait until the market reaches your price target, if there are signs that the market could turn again and you could give back the accumulated profit.

<u>Take what the market gives you</u>. That is simple, but hard to do. I have learned this simple rule the hard way. I have always been the hero waiting for the market to reach my target price instead of just taking the money that the market put on

the table. I had to learn to take this money, whether it was 50 dollars or 500 dollars.

Chapter 7: Does the Stop really protect me from heavy losses?

No matter how fast or how slow you want to get out of the trade, you can always sleep peacefully with bracket orders. Your risk is limited from the outset. Well... not quite. In volatile phases, and in particular because of sharp, sudden price drops, the execution price may differ significantly from the stop price. This is especially true if you hold a position overnight, or over the weekend. It is quite possible that a market opens on Monday morning with a substantial gap. If you trade leveraged instruments such as futures or forex, this can lead to significant losses and in extreme cases (such as the so-called "Francogeddon") to existence-threatening losses.

As already mentioned several times, the best insurance against this case is trading with small or "justifiable" positions. As a trader, you must always keep the worst-case scenario in mind. As a rule, in my experience, such losses and profits balance out in the course of a trader's career (the extreme movement can sometimes happen to your advantage, as it once happened to me in EUR/JPY during the Euro crisis). Within half an hour my position was 700 pips in profit! Sometimes you will be on the winning side, sometimes on the losing side.

However, on very rare occasions it can become dangerous. Then we talk about *black swan events*. These are events such as the aforementioned *Francogeddon*, in which the entire financial community was taken by surprise by an external event. In the case of the Francogeddon, the Swiss National

Bank lifted the Euro minimum exchange rate of 1.20 on 15 January 2015 without warning. The Swiss franc soared by almost 20 percent in one fell swoop.

Only a guaranteed stop-loss order helps against such an event. Here, the broker guarantees the closing of the position exactly to the desired price. The broker therefore bears the risk and must bear the costs of deviations himself. In return, the trader usually pays a fee for this guarantee. The fee can also be collected by widening the spreads. You must therefore consider this charge as a kind of insurance premium. Talk to your broker and ask him if he offers guaranteed stop-loss orders and what they cost.

It is at the discretion of the trader whether he wants to trade with guaranteed stops or not.

Concerning this topic, I have two remarks. First, as I said earlier, you should trade with appropriate positions so that, if such an event occurs, you will not be ruined right away. Second, in extreme cases, such as the Francogeddon, the broker took the loss even though he did not have to. This was the case with my broker. It is therefore quite important that you choose a broker who has survived such events as the Francogeddon and perhaps even stepped in for his customers who were on the "wrong side". Third, in the case of the snapback strategy, we are usually on the safe side, because "the disaster" has already happened. The strategy is designed to wait for the extreme movement and then take the opposite position. This fact alone is the best insurance against extreme price movements.

Incidentally, such extreme situations do not only occur on the short side. There are also cases of stocks that have risen so dramatically that those who held short positions were not only "grilled" but went bankrupt. Probably the most prominent example of such a "short squeeze" was the price of the German Volkswagen ordinary shares at the end of October 2008. On 26 October 2008, Volkswagen informed Porsche that it had increased its stake in Volkswagen from 35% to 42%. It had gained 6% and had secured a further 31.5% through options, resulting in a total stake of 74.1% in the full exercise of the option. However, many traders had bet on falling prices and shorted ordinary Volkswagen shares. Since the German state of Lower Saxony held another 20% of Volkswagen shares, less than 6% of the shares remained freely tradable. The short sellers, however, had borrowed 12% of the shares they had to buy to repatriate the loan on the stock market. Therefore, they were stuck in a short squeeze. By closing their short positions, the price of the common stock exploded and rose within two days from around 200 EUR to over 1,000 EUR!

This example shows you that the stock market can sometimes be a very irrational place. It is therefore important that as a trader, who in most cases acts like a hedge fund with leveraged products, you know what you are doing.

As far as the stop distance to the entry is concerned, I usually choose a generous stop. To return, for example, to the Bund Futures trade. If a market has gone up 600 points and I go short, hoping to catch at least 100 to 200 points of correction, then it makes no sense to work with a stop of 50 points. I hope you can see that. On the morning of May 29, the Bund Future alone soared 200 points, before reaching its final high. If you go short here, with a stop of 50 points, the chance of getting your stop hit from a last uprush of buyers is considerably high. It can work out, but the chance that you will be knocked out of the market is simply more likely than the chance of winning.

That is why I would choose a stop of at least 150 points in such movements. This kind stop is far away from the current market. Should this stop also be caught, it is usually a clear indication that your assessment is wrong and that the market will continue to rise.

Chapter 8: Trade Management

Concerning the management of the trade, we can keep it short. This is because we are relying on a snapback, i.e. a rebound of a price movement. As a rule, you will have to settle for 70 to 100 points. It could be more, but often these countermoves after an extreme movement are short. That is why you should take what the market gives you.

Although I have experimented with trailing stops, I could not find any benefit in it. It makes sense, however, to set the stop to breakeven as soon as you have 50-60 points profit. It just does not make sense to let the trade go into loss once you have made such a profit.

As I said, the best thing you can do is to take the money that is on the table and run. That may sound unorthodox, but it is mostly good for your account.

Chapter 9: Exit

Once you have come to the realization that it is impossible to find the perfect entry (unless by chance), this naturally also applies to the exit of the trade. Unlike the entry, I am not that patient at the exit. For example, if a trade is well into profit but has not yet reached the price target, I do not hesitate to take the profit if the market does not go beyond a certain level. The snapback method is about taking what the market gives you. If it takes too long to get beyond a certain level, I do not hesitate, and just take what I have.

Some traders will argue here, that you are trading suboptimally, because you are not exploiting the full potential of your trade. I understand this objection. However, it comes from a different trading philosophy that patiently places trades, and then lets the market decide whether it will hit the price target or the stop first.

If, regarding the entry, I wrote: trade only when you are scared, that would mean, for the exit: <u>and sell as soon as you feel the greed</u>.

Most traders do the opposite. They are impatient with the entry (they are greedy to buy or sell, no matter what) and then they are infinitely patient at the exit (they are afraid to close the position, even if the profit is not that big). With this strategy, you have to learn to take the money that is on the table and run.

So the snapback strategy is to wait patiently for a good chance and then hit it fast, like a sniper lying in wait a full day to fire a single shot. I cannot think of a better image for this strategy.

Chapter 10: When do the best trading opportunities occur?

Of course, that too is not set in stone, because good opportunities for this method can occur at any moment. Concerning the main markets, my experience shows that, in New York, they occur more frequently at noon or in the late afternoon, when the markets have reached daily lows or highs. You have to wait until you get a real chance. The reason is simple. If you have a strong trend in a market, and every trader is short, then you may not get into your countertrend position until the end of the day, when the day traders close out their positions.

Often, this is a good time to act. You must always keep in mind that if the market has made a trend day (the market has gone in a certain direction), then those who have traded this trend are sitting on profits, which they eventually will take at the end of the day. This fact alone causes pressure in the opposite direction, which is why this is often the best moment to apply the snapback method.

Chapter 11: Why you should study the economic calendar

An important (and often underestimated) ability of a trader is the correct assessment of the so-called economic calendar. I like to use the calendar of the website forexfactory.com.

Image 6: Economic calendar of December 12, 2018

Date	5:08am	Currency	Impact		Detail	Actual	Forecast	Previous	Graph
Wed Dec 12	12:27am	AUD	■	Westpac Consumer Sentiment		0.1%		2.8%	
	12:50am	JPY	□	Core Machinery Orders m/m		7.6%	10.2%	-18.3%	
		JPY	□	PPI y/y		2.3%	2.4%	3.0%	
	5:30am	JPY	□	Tertiary Industry Activity m/m		1.9%	0.9%	-1.2%	
	10:00am	EUR	□	Italian Quarterly Unemployment Rate			10.3%	10.7%	
	11:00am	EUR	□	Industrial Production m/m			0.2%	-0.3%	
	2:30pm	CAD	□	Capacity Utilization Rate			85.9%	85.5%	
		USD	■	CPI m/m			0.0%	0.3%	
		USD	■	Core CPI m/m			0.2%	0.2%	
	4:30pm	USD	□	Crude Oil Inventories			-3.3M	-7.3M	
	7:01pm	USD	□	10-y Bond Auction				3.21|2.5	
	8:00pm	USD	□	Federal Budget Balance			-193.5b	-100.5B	
	10:45pm	NZD	□	PPI m/m				-0.9%	

The color of the small icon in the form of a small factory gives you an indication of the importance of the expected event. Forexfactory works with three colors: yellow, orange and red. Yellow and orange icons indicate that the numbers are not that important, at least not in order to move the market significantly. If the factory icon is red, this generally means that the event is considered important and that you can expect increased volatility (i.e. trading opportunities). In the example in Image 6, there was only one significant event on that day: US consumer prices at 8:30 am. Consumer prices accounted for much of the total headline inflation. Inflation is important for currency valuation as the Fed could raise interest rates due to rising prices.

A significant movement can occur, particularly if the figures deviate significantly from expectations. The analysts' forecast for the day was 0.0%. That means, the majority of analysts expected no change in consumer prices. This prognosis turned out to be correct. The analysts' numbers were confirmed. Of course, you look at how the dollar will react in such an event, so you open the EUR/USD chart. If the figures are in line with expectations, there will usually be no major movement, because all the information was priced on the market in advance. Except for a little twitch, the market barely moved on that December 12th.

Conversely, an event that was only put into yellow by the forexfactory team (which means it was considered to be of less importance) could cause a near landslide move in a market. Of course, this usually happens when the actual numbers are so far beyond the expectations that the actors involved in this market are really startled.

The economic calendar is therefore not an exact forecasting tool. It merely tells you whether or not an important event is imminent. I am always amazed at how few traders include the economic calendar in their considerations. For example, some traders wonder why the markets barely move from Monday to Wednesday, and are trading in tight spots. If I ask them why this is so, they shrug their shoulders, though everyone should know that the ECB's interest rate decision was due on Thursday that week. If important economic or monetary policy decisions do not move the financial markets, what will?

Therefore, you should study the calendar at the beginning of the week and take some notes. For example, if we expect unemployment figures in New Zealand, then perhaps you should look at the NZD/USD that day. Should I, as a trader, be interested in the unemployment figures in New Zealand? The answer is yes. Here they are:

Image 7: Unemployment figures New Zealand 2000 – 2018

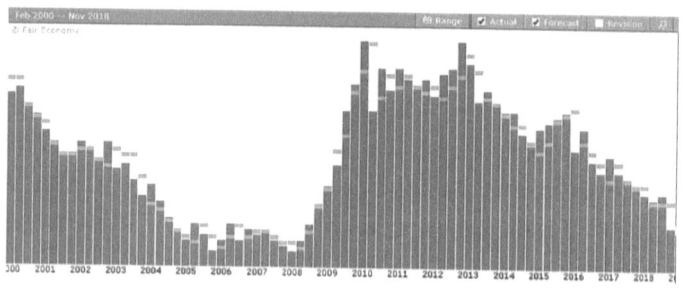

You can find this graph by clicking on the small brown button next to the event on forexfactory. Then, a window opens with an explanation of the event. Right under the term "history", you will see "graph". Click on it to see how the numbers have developed over the past few quarters. We can clearly see how the unemployment rate increased significantly during the course of the 2008 financial crisis. In the following years, the New Zealand economy was able to recover. The unemployment rate (at the end of 2018) is now approaching the good figures of before the financial crisis.

On November 6, the unemployment rate (35 days after the end of each quarter) was announced. The previous quota was 4.4%. The analysts' expectation was that the ratio would again be 4.4%. However, the numbers were much better than expected, as they came in well below, at 3.9%. The reaction of the market players came immediately:

Image 8: NZDUSD, hourly chart November 2 to November 7

As you can see on the chart, the market was very quiet in the days before the numbers. There was hardly any movement. Apparently, the market players liked the new unemployment rate, because immediately after the announcement, the New Zealand dollar shot up 70 pips. I say "apparently", because one can assume the causal chain "less unemployed - good for the economy - good for the currency". However, this causal chain is by no means always sure.

Would such a move upwards be sufficient for me to go short here? Honestly not. That is a nice move in this pair, but that is not what I would call an "extreme movement", because then the pair would have to move several percentage points, or several hundred pips in one direction. And that was clearly not the case here. The market reacted positively to these good figures within the expected range. But no more.

Chapter 12: Which markets are suitable for the snapback strategy?

In principle, this strategy can be implemented in any tradable market. It is important that the market you choose to trade in is liquid enough so that you can quickly get out of a position if necessary. Here is an overview of the markets that I like to trade:

Currencies: EUR/USD, EUR/JPY, AUD/USD, NZD/USD, USD/JPY, GBP/JPY, USD/CHF, USD/CAD, GBP/CHF, AUD/JPY, EUR/CHF

Indices: Dow Jones, NASDAQ, SP500, DAX, CAC40, Eurostoxx50, Nikkei 225

Bonds: Bund Future, BOBL Future, 30 Year US Bond, 10 Year Note

Precious metals: gold, silver, platinum, palladium

Commodities: Copper, WTI, Brent, Natural Gas, Wheat, Corn, Cocoa, Cotton, Orange Juice, Coffee, Sugar

Equities: Mostly US equities with a market capitalization of at least $ 2 billion.

These are my usual markets, but of course, everyone is free to add more markets to this list. It may sometimes be interesting to trade markets you would normally not trade. During the so-called "Italian crisis", I traded futures on Italian bonds. Alternatively, in the weeks leading up to the Brexit vote, I traded the FTSE 100, which I normally do not trade.

There are always opportunities when you look around the world with open eyes and ears and occasionally think outside the box.

Part 2: Trading Examples

Chapter 1: Examples in the Stock Indices

Image 9: FDAX, hourly chart

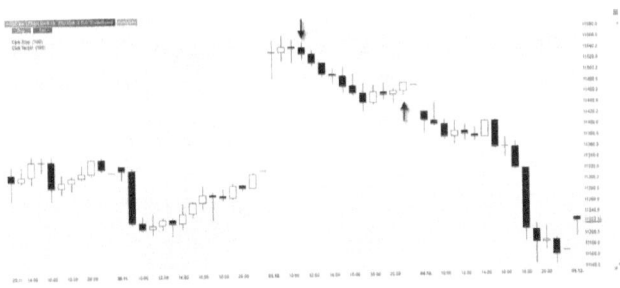

In this example, the DAX Future opened on Monday morning of December 3, 2018 with a gap up of more than 200 points. A very enthusiastic opening, I thought, screaming for a correction. After the market had been in the 11,530 - 11,550 range for about 2 hours, without any further increase, I opted for a short position (red arrow above). My assumption was confirmed. The FDAX actually began to fall, but without big steps down. Overall, I had slightly less than 100 points profit in the evening. The gap had still not closed by then. However, I wanted to be on the safe side, and took the profit (small black arrow on the right). As you can see, this decision was a bit premature, because the next morning the FDAX opened with a small gap down. During the day, the futures continued to fall until they finally closed the Monday's gap and fell even lower. Overall, I could have made over 400 points with this trade if I had stayed in the position. This is also the criticism of my method: I act suboptimally, so to speak, if I leave so many points on the table.

Only, how could I possibly have known, on the evening of December 3, that the FDAX would continue falling the next morning? I could not know it by any means. Nobody knew it. Sometimes gaps are closed immediately, but sometimes you can wait months until it happens. The only thing I really "knew" was that a correction after such a gap-up was likely, which eventually happened. Although I could have guessed that the gap would be closed the next day, I decided to take what the market had given so far. I think that is an important principle that many have a hard time with: take what the market gives you and leave. To speculate whether one should stay in there, because more could possibly come, is simply pointless. You cannot know. Remember, the snapback method is a _reaction to an extreme movement_. Unfortunately, the extent to which the market can extend this reaction is not predictable, so I think that it is generally better to close the position.

Image 10: Dow Jones Mini Future, Hourly Chart, October 8 – 16, 2018

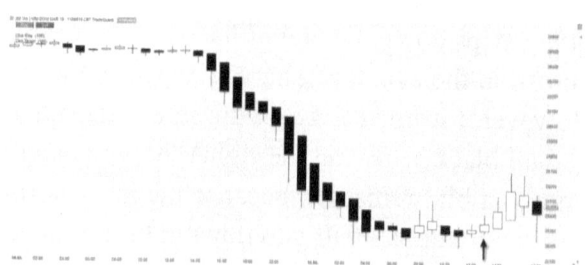

On October 10, the Dow Jones Future fell over 1,000 points. As you can see in the heikin ashi chart, there was hardly any significant countermovement. Therefore, the snapback trader had to be patient. The low of the move was 25,188 points which was reached in the early morning of the next day. Only, in the European morning a significant countermovement occurred (arrow below), which sent the future to over 450 points back north. A skilled trader could have realized more than 200 points here.

Of course, such moves rarely occur, but they are worth trading, because the "technical corrections" usually bring in over a hundred points.

Chapter 2. Examples in the Currency Markets (Forex)

Image 11: GBP/JPY, 4-hour chart, September - November 2018

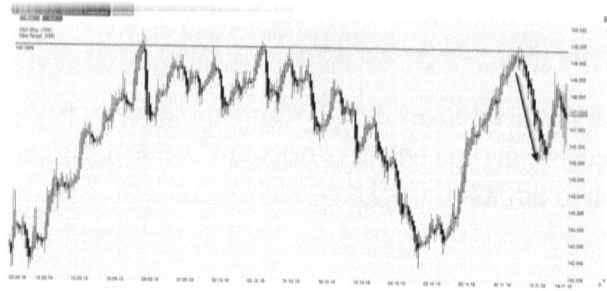

In this example, the market presented a gift, which happens from time to time. At least, I considered it a gift. As you can see, during the month of September, GBP/JPY failed repeatedly to conquer a resistance at 149.28 (horizontal line above). Overall, the market ran into the resistance on four occasions, but was repeatedly rejected by the sellers. Since these attempts were all based on small movements, there was no need for action here. Finally, GBP/JPY fell back over the next month, reaching support at 143.00. However, the pair began to rise again on November 1, 2018, and has now formed an uptrend that was barely accompanied by significant corrections. The heikin ashi mode of the chart nicely illustrates this fact by charting the uptrend with lots of green candles (green arrow). Overall, the pair rallied over 5,000 pips, until it finally regained the resistance at 149.28.

Image 12: GBPJPY, hourly chart, 11.8.2018

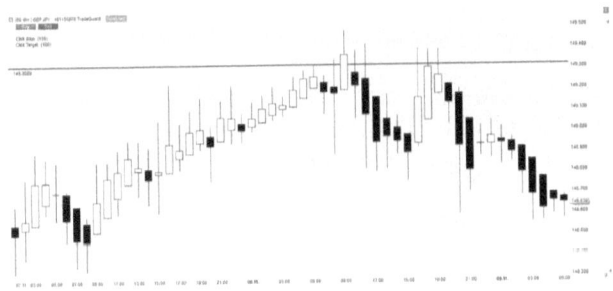

We see, on the hourly chart, that the pair reached the resistance in the early morning of November 8. At around 9:00 am, there was a first unsuccessful attempt to overcome the resistance. The pair stayed below the resistance in the hours that followed. Here, of course, you could build a first short position, unless you wait for the confirmation, which would come a few hours later. The problem is, as in this case, there can always be a second unsuccessful attempt to overcome the resistance, and only then will you receive your confirmation. However, it could just as well be that the pair starts to fall immediately after the first failure. No matter how you want to do it, you will repeatedly experience that the market will decide differently than you expected. Sometimes, as in this example, the market will try to overcome the resistance twice, sometimes it will turn right away and start to run in the other direction, and of course, the market can overcome the resistance, if necessary after several attempts. Therefore, if you get this signal, you should just go short. Sometimes your position will run into profit, and sometimes you will have to wait a few hours. However, if you see a strong movement (shouting for a correction) and the movement stops at a strong resistance, then you get the trade almost as a gift.

Over the next few days, the pair fell over 3,000 points, as shown in Image 11.

Image 13: GBPUSD, hourly chart, September 17- 29, 2018

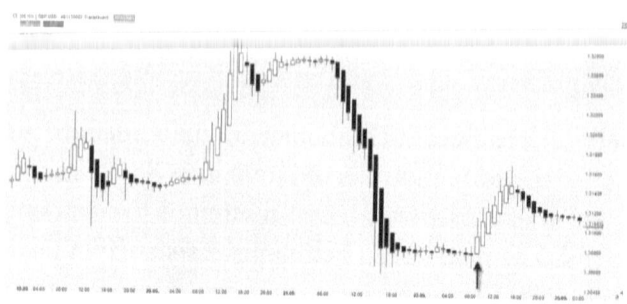

This example of the British pound is exemplary. On Friday, September 21, the pound had dropped over 200 pips. It was not a huge move, but at least a decent crash after the previous day's winnings. The pair reached its lows in the late afternoon and traded sideways in the evening hours, in a narrow range. Of course, it is always risky to take a position before the weekend. I prefer to wait until after the weekend to get in. Indeed, the "technical countermovement" happened on Monday morning. A snapback trader could make 50 to 60 pips in this move.

As you can see, you should adjust your profit target in this strategy to the previous movement. To expect a correction of 150 pips with a previous movement of 200 pips is very ambitious. After a move of 200 pips, you might expect a correction of 50 or 60 pips. The stop should be at least 100 points away.

Chapter 3: Examples in the stock markets

Image 14: Weight Watchers, 15-minute chart, November 1-6, 2018

Weight Watchers (NASDAQ: WTW) shares opened on November 2, 2018 with a gap down of over $ 14. The stock fell further in the first half hour and lost almost another $ 8. Overall, the stock dropped more than 30% in one day. WTW plummeted after management announced that the number of subscribers to Weight Watchers had dropped further and that the company had missed sales expectations in the third quarter. The stock fell below $ 48 half an hour after it opened, even though it was on $ 68 the previous night. Of course, 30% in one day is a proper bloodletting. However, for a snapback trader looking for a quick fix, it was a chance to take some points in that stock. As you can see on the chart, this "technical correction" came after about an hour (arrow below). Those who watched the stock could perhaps get in at $ 48.50 and sell at $ 51 after about 45 minutes. This may seem like peanuts to some, but these peanuts represent 5.15% in one stock in less than an hour. This is hard to achieve with conventional day trading in stocks. However, in the case of a dramatic crash of a stock and the associated volatility, you might get similarly quick returns. I would have set the stop here at about $ 46.50, which is $ 2 lower than my entry, knowing that this stop could be caught anytime, which did not happen in this case.

Image 15: Green Sky, 15-minute chart

The stock of Green Sky Inc. (GSKY) fell 38% on the morning of November 6, after failing to meet September quarter sales expectations and posting a negative forecast for the next quarter. As you can see, this message was not to the liking of the market players at all. In the first trading hour, the stock fell further, from $ 10 to $ 8.80. Then some buyers appeared. A snapback trader could buy at $ 9 (small green arrow on the left). However, this purchase would have been too early, because the stock sank to $ 8.55 again in the next half hour. The correction came after this second dip. The position would have gone into the red first, but it recovered and finally ran into profit (big green arrow). The trader was able to sell the stock at about $ 9.50. After all, that would have been a gain of 5.50% in two hours. However, you have to be fast and ready to take what the market offers you. As this example shows, you should not assume that you will always buy at the low. For that reason alone, I recommend smaller positions and more generous stops. In that case, the stop could have been around $ 8.50. With these types of trades, you will not achieve good risk reward ratios. You should try to get at least a RRR of 1:1. If you risk a dollar, you should also try to get one. Ultimately, it is the hit rate, that is relatively high in this method, which will give you the profit.

In the case of Green Sky, we see that the stock traded in a range between $ 9 and $ 9.50 for the remainder of the day. My experience is that it is best to get in at the first recovery. Later recoveries and buying waves are not as reliable anymore.

Image 16: Signet Jewelers, 5-minute chart

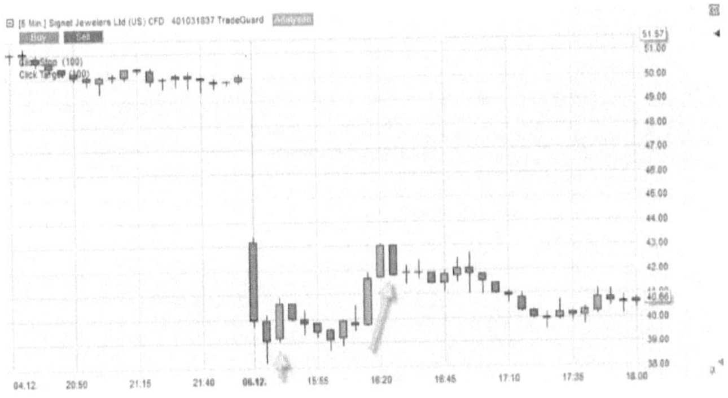

In the case of the Signet Jewelers, the stock went from $ 50 to $ 40 on December 6 – a crash of 20%. The jewelry chain reported a quarterly loss of $ 29.9 million, or $ 1.06 per share. In the first few minutes of the trading the day, the stock fell to almost $ 38, then the first buyers appeared, as you can see from the third candle, which was bullish. For example, if you bought here for $ 40, you also had to wait about half an hour for the correction. The stock fell below $ 39 again. After that, the buyers came in and drove the stock back to $ 43. Let us assume you got out at $ 42 – you would have made 5% profit here in one hour.

Chapter 4. Examples in the commodity markets

Image 17: Natural Gas, November 14, 2018, hourly chart

The commodity markets offer the best opportunities for snapback traders, because sometimes huge movements can occur in a short amount of time, which is rare in currencies or indices. Look at this upward movement in the natural gas future. The market had stayed sideways longer in the $ 3.20 range. On November 2, it broke out of this range and then quoted at about $ 3.50, a good thirty cents higher. In the following days, Natural Gas continued to quote higher, eventually rising more than 60 cents within two hours on November 14. Overall, the market rose by 50% in less than 2 weeks! On the evening of November 14, the future even reached $ 4.90 in a second move.

Image 18: Natural gas, November 14, 15-minute chart

As the picture clearly shows, you could already have made a decent profit during the first movement, because the market corrected by 50 cents! These are huge intraday movements, sometimes over 10%. I think it speaks for itself that, as a trader, you have to adjust your position size when you trade that kind of market.

In the evening, the second wave came, which again led in the direction of $ 4.90. Then, when the future could not overcome this resistance, for me it was a clear short signal (small arrow above). I only had to wait until the next day for the correction. In a few hours, the future fell from $ 4.80back to $ 4.00. That is a gain of over 16%. You will not get that often, but as you see, it is possible.

Image 19: Wheat Future, hourly chart, 11.6 - 12.10.2018

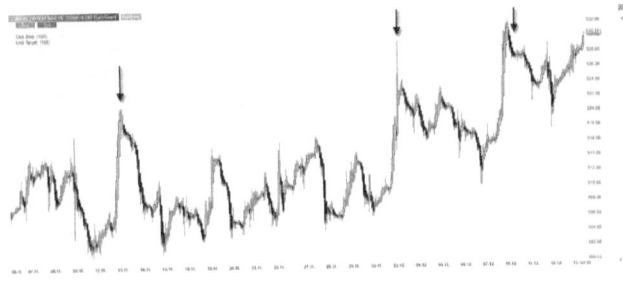

Wheat is also a commodity that I like to trade. You can count on the fact that there are always exaggerations (up and down) that can be traded well. This example in the hourly chart illustrates this very well. Again, it is best to compress the chart so that you can see the exaggerations at a glance. At that time, wheat oscillated in a range of $ 5 to $ 10, but there were three exaggerations up (red arrows), which, for me, were a clear invitation to go short. Does it always work? No! However, it works quite often and that is enough. As you can see, about every other week you get a chance like this, if you follow this market.

Glossary

Automated or algorithmic trading: Indicates the automatic trading of securities by computer programs

Black Swan: An unforeseen event that gives economic development a decisive turn

Broker: Financial service provider who is responsible for the execution of securities investors' orders

Bund Future: German Term contract, which refers to a notional, long-term German federal bond, with a coupon of 6 percent and a maturity of 10 years

Candlestick: Coding of price changes on the basis of a Japanese analysis technology

DAX: main German stock index

Day trading: Day trading describes the short-term speculative trading of securities. Positions are opened and closed again within the same trading day, with the aim of benefiting from low price fluctuations

Drawdown: Losses that can arise out of the peak within a certain time

E-Mini Futures: Futures contract on the American index SP500

Entry Strategy: A strategy that determines the entry into a market

Exit Strategy: A strategy that determines the exit from a market

Exponential Moving Average: Exponential moving averages (EMAs) reduce the lag in the formation of the average price by giving more weight to recent prices

Forex: Forex Exchange Market, international currency market.

Francogeddon: On 15 January 2015, the Swiss National Bank lifted the minimum euro exchange rate of 1.20 without warning. The Swiss franc increased in price by almost 20 percent

Futures: Futures contract. Standardized contract to buy or sell a specific amount of a commodity at a specified price, on a specified date

Gap: A gap between two trading days

Heikin Ashi: "balancing on one foot" Japanese representation form of price changes

Hit ratio: Describes the ratio of profit trades to loss trades

Indicator: Identification of technical analysis, which is designed to determine price movements of securities

Liquidity: Describes the extent to which a security can be sold and bought at any given time

Long: To be Long; having purchased securities and thus be the owner of the securities

Market Efficiency Hypothesis: According to this theory, financial markets are efficient insofar as existing information is already priced in and thus no market participant is able to achieve above-average profits through technical analysis, fundamental analysis, insider trading or otherwise

Mean-reversion: The tendency of a financial market to return to its average after an extreme position

Money management: A value-added strategy that aims at controlling the risk of a securities portfolio by setting the size of the individual trading positions

Moving Average: moving average indicator

Pennystocks: shares whose value is less than one dollar in the local currency

Pip: Percentage in point, the smallest change in the price in currency trading

Risk Management: Includes all measures for the systematic identification, analysis, assessment, monitoring and control of risks

Risk reward ratio (RRR): The RRR serves as an indicator of the meaningfulness of a trade. It is calculated by dividing the expected profitability by the greatest possible loss (stop loss)

Scalping: Trading technique, in which the trader tries to trade minimal movements in the market

Short position: A trader short is when he sells a position without owning them (short sale)

Short Squeeze: Shortage of supply of a security that has been previously shorted in large numbers

Simple Moving Average: A simple moving average is formed by calculating the average price of a security over a specified number of periods

Slippage: The difference between the estimated and the actual price of an asset purchase

S&P 500 (Standard & Poor's 500): A stock index comprising 500 of the largest listed American companies

Stock index: Indicator of the performance of the stock market as a whole or of individual stock groups (eg Dow Jones Industrials)

Stop Loss Order: Sell order which is carried out once a certain price is reached

Take profit order: Automated order, triggered as soon as a predefined price target has been reached

Target price: Stock market price that a security is to achieve on the basis of an analysis

Trailing Stop: An automatic stop loss order

Trend following: Trading strategy, which is based on following a once identified trend

Volatility: Standard deviation. Indicates how much a price fluctuates

Other Books by Heikin Ashi Trader

How to start a Trading Business with $500

Many new traders have little capital available in the beginning, but this is not an obstacle to starting a trading career anyway.

However, this book is not about how to grow a $500 account into a $500,000 account. It is precisely these exaggerated return expectations that bring most beginners to failure.

Instead, the author shows, in a realistic way, how you can become a full-time trader in spite of limited start-up capital. This applies both for traders who want to remain private, as well as for those who want to eventually trade customer funds.

This book shows step by step how to do it. In addition, there is a concrete action plan for each step. Anyone can be a trader in principle, if he or she is willing to learn how this business works.

How to Scalp the Mini DAX Futures

Thanks to the introduction of the Mini-DAX futures (FDXM) private traders with smaller accounts are afforded the opportunity to scalp the German DAX Index to professional terms. Unlike most other trading instruments, Futures are the most transparent and effective way to make money in the financial markets.

Scalpers have infinitely more trading opportunities than position traders or day traders, which constitutes the real strength of this trading style. A scalper may therefore manage his capital much more effectively than all other market participants and thus achieve much greater returns than would otherwise be the case.

The Heikin Ashi Trader shows in this book how to successfully scalp this new future on the DAX. You will learn how to enter the market, how to manage your position and at which point you should back out. In addition, the book contains a wealth of tips and tools to make your trading even more effective and precise.

About the Author

Heikin Ashi Trader is recognized worldwide as the specialist in scalping with the Heikin Ashi chart. He has been trading this way for 19 years. He traded for a hedge fund and then went into business for himself as a trader. His scalping book "Scalping is Fun!" is an international bestseller and has been sold more than 30,000 times. You can find more information about his scalping method on his website www.heikinashitrader.net

Imprint

Copyright © 2019 by Heikin Ashi Trader

All rights reserved. No part of this book may be reproduced or utilized in any form or by any means, electronic or mechanical, including photocopying, recording, or by any information storage and retrieval system, without written permission of the publisher.

First edition, February 2019

The information presented herein represents the view of the author as of the date of publication. This book is presented for informational and entertainment purposes only. Due to the rate at which economic and cultural conditions change, the author reserves the right to alter and update his opinions based on new conditions. While every attempt has been made to verify the information in this book, neither the author nor his affiliates/partners assume any responsibility for errors, inaccuracies, or omissions. At no time shall the information contained herein be constructed as professional, investment, tax, accounting, legal or medical advice. This book does not constitute a recommendation or a warrant of suitability for any particular business, industry, website, security, portfolio of securities, transaction, or investment strategy.

Published by:

Dao Press

Dao Press is an imprint of Splendid Island, Ltd.
Scanbox # 05927
Ehrenbergstr 16a
10245 Berlin - Deutschland
All Rights Reserved

www.ingramcontent.com/pod-product-compliance
Lightning Source LLC
Chambersburg PA
CBHW030940240526
45463CB00015B/858